Contents

Straight

These pieces of spaghetti are all **straight**.

straight

How Do Things Move?

Straight and Curving

Sue Barraclough

www.heinemann.co.uk/library
Visit our website to find out more information about **Heinemann Library** books.

To order:
Phone 44 (0) 1865 888066
Send a fax to 44 (0) 1865 314091
Visit the Heinemann Bookshop at www.heinemann.co.uk/library to browse our catalogue and order online.

First published in Great Britain by Heinemann Library, Halley Court, Jordan Hill, Oxford OX2 8EJ, part of Harcourt Education. Heinemann is a registered trademark of Harcourt Education Ltd.

ery and

s) Pte. Ltd
China

10 digit ISBN 0 431 02426 X (hardback)
13 digit ISBN 978 0 431 02426 4 (hardback)
11 10 09 08 07 06
10 9 8 7 6 5 4 3 2 1
10 digit ISBN 0 431 02431 6 (paperback)
13 digit ISBN 978 0 431 02431 8 (paperback)

11 10 09 08 07
10 9 8 7 6 5 4 3 2 1

British Library Cataloguing in Publication Data
Barraclough, Sue
Straight and curving. - (How do things move?)
1.Momentum (Mechanics) - Juvenile literature
I.Title
531.1'12
A full catalogue record for this book is available from the British Library.

Acknowledgements
The publishers would like to thank the following for permission to reproduce photographs: Alamy Images pp. **11, 23 top left** (Bertrand Collet), **13** (Royalty-Free), **16** (Stockbyte Platinum); Corbis pp. **4, 8**; Corbis pp. **12, 20, 22 top right, 23 top right** (Royalty free), **15, 22 bottom** (Ariel Skelley), **18** (Tom Stewart), **21, 23 bottom** (Robert Pickett); Digital Vision p. **9** (Robert Harding World Imagery/Jim Reed); Getty Images pp. **5, 6, 7** (Photodisc); Harcourt Education Ltd (Tudor Photography) pp. **14, 22 top left**; Photographers Direct p. **17** (Skyscan); Superstock p. **10** (Raymond Forbes); Trip p. **19** (Art Directors).

Cover photograph reproduced with permission of Alamy (Epictura).

Every effort has been made to contact copyright holders of any material reproduced in this book. Any omissions will be rectified in subsequent printings if notice is given to the publishers.

The paper used to print this book comes from sustainable resources.

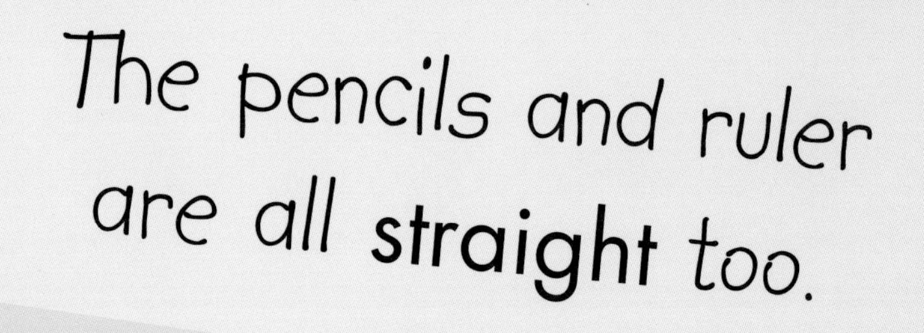

The pencils and ruler are all **straight** too.

Curved

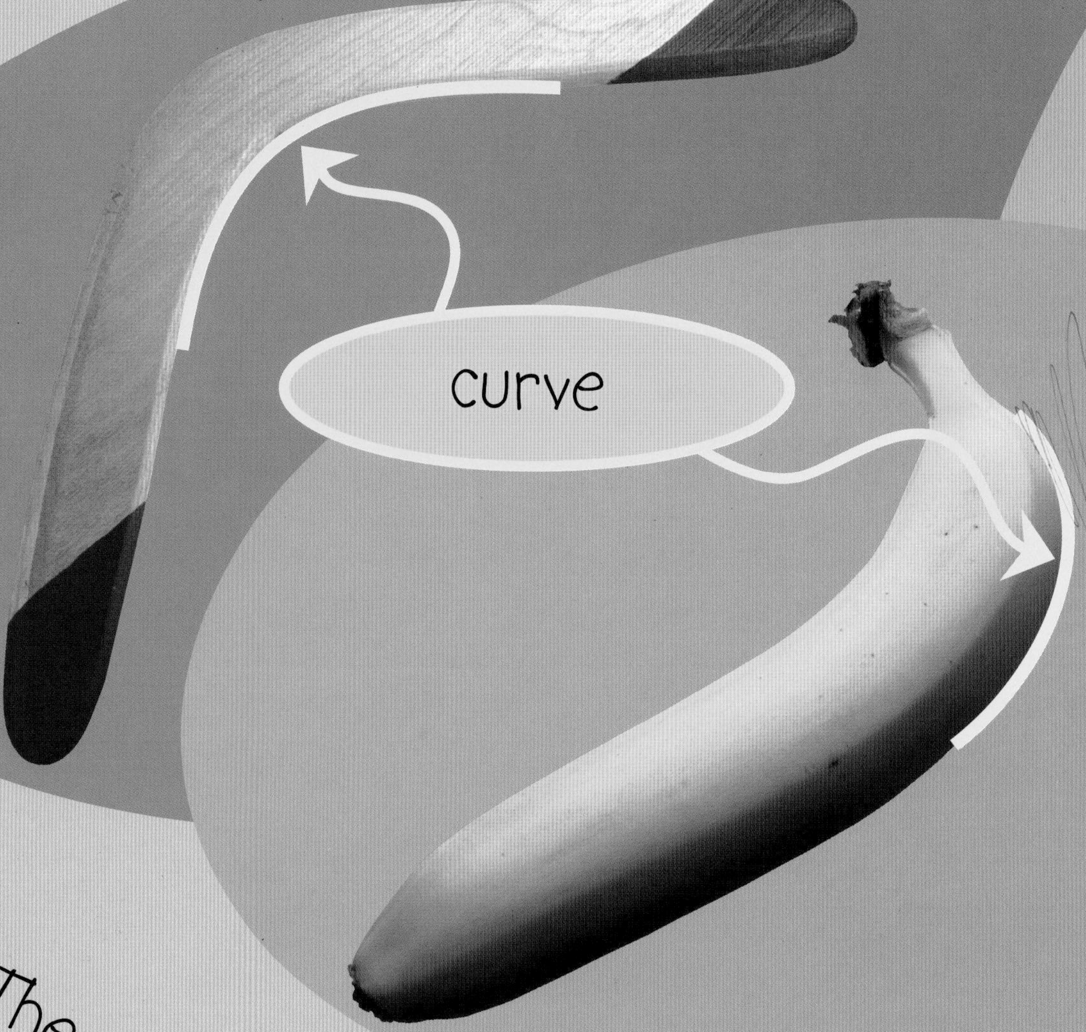

curve

These things are both **curved**.

Can you follow the **curves** on this bridge with your finger?

Straight and curved

Are these flagpoles straight or **curved**?

Is this rainbow **straight** or **curved**?

Moving straight

This car is going **straight** along the road.

These aeroplanes are flying **straight** in the sky.

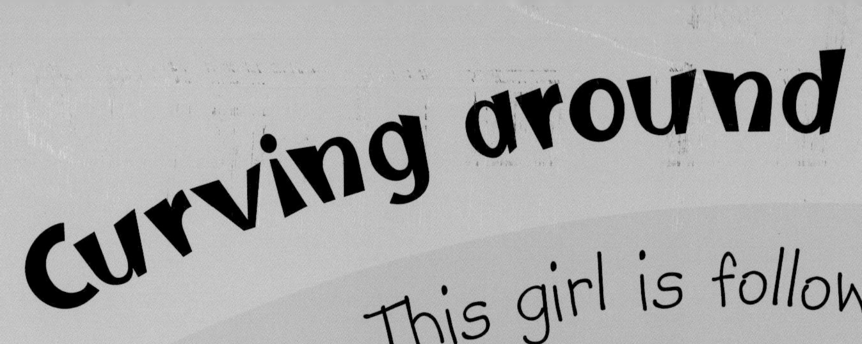

Curving around

This girl is following the **curve** in the path.

This skateboarder is zooming around the **curves** in the path.

Sliding down

This slide is **straight**.

The girl is going **straight** down the slide.

This slide has many **curves**.

The girl is **curving** down the slide.

Up in the sky

This kite is flying high in the sky.

Is it flying **straight?**

Is this kite flying straight or is it curving?

Fun and games

This girl is sliding down the pole.
Is she moving straight?

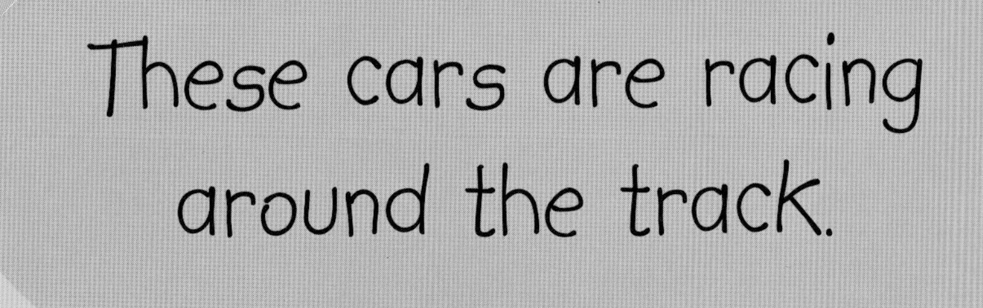
These cars are racing around the track.

Are they moving straight or are they curving?

Plants and animals

This sunflower is growing tall and strong.

Is it growing **straight**?

This worm is moving along the ground.
Is it moving straight or is it curving?

Straight or curving?

Can you remember which things move **straight** and which things **curve**?

Index

Notes for adults

The *How Do Things Move?* series provides young children with a first opportunity to learn about motion. Each book encourages children to notice and ask questions about the types of movement they see around them. The following Early Learning Goals are relevant to the series:

Knowledge and understanding of the world

- Find out about and identify some features of living things and objects
- Ask questions about why things happen and how things work
- Show an interest in the world in which they live
- Encourage use of evaluative and comparative language

These books will also help children extend their vocabulary, as they will hear some new words. Since words are used in context in the book this should enable young children to gradually incorporate them into their own vocabulary.

Follow-up activities

- Reinforce the concepts of straight and curved by asking your child to identify three objects in the room with curves, and three objects with straight lines.
- Encourage your child to think further about moving in a straight or curved line by asking them to decide which would be quicker to get from A to B. Then get them to test their theory by running across the room.